HAL•LEONARD

VIOLIN
PLAY-ALONG

BLUES CLASSICS

ISBN 978-1-4234-8646-6

HAL•LEONARD®
CORPORATION

7777 W. BLUEMOUND RD. P.O. BOX 13819 MILWAUKEE, WI 53213

Recorded and Produced by Dan Maske

Jerry Loughney, Violin

Visit Hal Leonard Online at
www.halleonard.com

CONTENTS

Dust My Broom

Words and Music by Elmore James and Robert Johnson

Additional Lyrics

2. I'm gonna write a letter, telephone every town I know.
   I'm gonna write a letter, telephone every town I know.
   If I don't find her in Mississippi, she's over in Westminster, I know.

3. And I don't want no woman want every downtown man she meets.
   Now, I don't want no woman want every downtown man she meets.
   Means she a no-good, dirty... they shouldn't allow her on the street.

4. I believe, I believe my time ain't long.
   I believe, I believe my time ain't long.
   I'm gonna leave my baby and break up my happy home.

Boom Boom

Words and Music by John Lee Hooker

Additional Lyrics

3. Won't you walk that walk and talk that talk?
   And whisper in my ear, tell me that you love me.
   I love that talk when you talk like that.
   You knocks me out, right off of my feet.
   Whoa, ho, ho, ho.

Born Under a Bad Sign

Words and Music by Booker T. Jones and William Bell

Hide Away

By Freddie King and Sonny Thompson

Killing Floor

Words and Music by Chester Burnett

Additional Lyrics

2. If I had a followed my first mind,
   If I had a followed my first mind,
   I'd a been gone since my second time.

3. I should have went on when my friend come from Mexico at me.
   I should have went on when my friend come from Mexico at me.
   But now I'm foolin' with you, baby, I let you put me on the killing floor.

4. God knows I should have been gone.
   God knows I should have been gone.
   Then I wouldn't have been here, down on the killing floor.

I'm Your Hoochie Coochie Man

Written by Willie Dixon

Well, _ you know I'm the Hoo-chie Coo-chie Man, _ ev - 'ry-bod-y knows I'm here. _

Violin Solo

the whole _ round world knows I'm here.

Additional Lyrics

2. I got a black cat bone,
   I got a mojo too.
   I got the John the Conquerroot,
   I'm gonna mess with you.
   I'm gonna make you girls
   Lead me by my hand.
   Then the world'll know
   I'm the Hoochie Coochie man.
   Chorus

3. On the seventh hour,
   On the seventh day,
   On the seventh month,
   The seventh doctor say,
   "You were born for good luck,
   And that you'll see."
   I got seven hundred dollars,
   Don't you mess with me.
   Chorus

My Babe

Written by Willie Dixon

Begin fade

Fade Out

Rock Me Baby

Words and Music by B.B. King and Joe Bihari

Additional Lyrics

2. Roll me, baby, like you roll a wagon wheel.
   Want you to roll me, baby, like you roll a wagon wheel.
   Want you to roll me, baby, you don't know how it makes me feel.

3. Rock me, baby, honey, rock me slow.
   Hey, rock me, pretty baby. Baby, rock me slow.
   Want you to rock me, baby, 'til I want no more.

PLAY MORE OF YOUR FAVORITE SONGS

WITH GREAT INSTRUMENTAL PLAY ALONG PACKS FROM HAL LEONARD

Ballads

Solo arrangements of 12 songs: Bridge Over Troubled Water • Bring Him Home • Candle in the Wind • Don't Cry for Me Argentina • I Don't Know How to Love Him • Imagine • Killing Me Softly with His Song • Nights in White Satin • Wonderful Tonight • more.

00841445	Flute	$10.95
00841446	Clarinet	$10.95
00841447	Alto Sax	$10.95
00841448	Tenor Sax	$10.95
00841449	Trumpet	$10.95
00841450	Trombone	$10.95
00841451	Violin	$10.95

Band Jam

12 band favorites complete with accompaniment CD, including: Born to Be Wild • Get Ready for This • I Got You (I Feel Good) • Rock & Roll – Part II (The Hey Song) • Twist and Shout • We Will Rock You • Wild Thing • Y.M.C.A • and more.

00841232	Flute	$10.95
00841233	Clarinet	$10.95
00841234	Alto Sax	$10.95
00841235	Trumpet	$10.95
00841236	Horn	$10.95
00841237	Trombone	$10.95
00841238	Violin	$10.95

Disney Movie Hits

Now solo instrumentalists can play along with a dozen favorite songs from Disney blockbusters, including: Beauty and the Beast • Circle of Life • Cruella De Vil • Go the Distance • God Help the Outcasts • Kiss the Girl • When She Loved Me • A Whole New World • and more.

00841420	Flute	$12.95
00841421	Clarinet	$12.95
00841422	Alto Sax	$12.95
00841423	Trumpet	$12.95
00841424	French Horn	$12.95
00841425	Trombone/Baritone	$12.95
00841686	Tenor Sax	$12.95
00841687	Oboe	$12.95
00841688	Mallet Percussion	$12.95
00841426	Violin	$12.95
00841427	Viola	$12.95
00841428	Cello	$12.95

Prices, contents, and availability subject to change without notice.
Disney characters and artwork © Disney Enterprises, Inc.

Disney Solos

An exciting collection of 12 solos with full-band accompaniment on CD. Songs include: Be Our Guest • Can You Feel the Love Tonight • Colors of the Wind • Reflection • Under the Sea • You've Got a Friend in Me • Zero to Hero • and more.

00841404	Flute	$12.95
00841405	Clarinet/Tenor Sax	$12.95
00841406	Alto Sax	$12.95
00841407	Horn	$12.95
00841408	Trombone	$12.95
00841409	Trumpet	$12.95
00841410	Violin	$12.95
00841411	Viola	$12.95
00841412	Cello	$12.95
00841506	Oboe	$12.95
00841553	Mallet Percussion	$12.95

Easy Disney Favorites

13 Disney favorites for solo instruments: Bibbidi-Bobbidi-Boo • It's a Small World • Let's Go Fly a Kite • Mickey Mouse March • A Spoonful of Sugar • Toyland March • Winnie the Pooh • The Work Song • Zip-A-Dee-Doo-Dah • and many more.

00841371	Flute	$12.95
00841477	Clarinet	$12.95
00841478	Alto Sax	$12.95
00841479	Trumpet	$12.95
00841480	Trombone	$12.95
00841372	Violin	$12.95
00841481	Viola	$12.95
00841482	Cello/Bass	$12.95

Favorite Movie Themes

13 themes, including: *An American Symphony* from Mr. Holland's Opus • Braveheart • Chariots of Fire • Forrest Gump – Main Title • Theme from *Jurassic Park* • Mission: Impossible Theme • and more.

00841166	Flute	$10.95
00841167	Clarinet	$10.95
00841168	Trumpet/Tenor Sax	$10.95
00841169	Alto Sax	$10.95
00841170	Trombone	$10.95
00841171	F Horn	$10.95
00841296	Violin	$10.95

Jazz & Blues

14 songs: Cry Me a River • Fever • Fly Me to the Moon • God Bless' the Child • Harlem Nocturne • Moonglow • A Night in Tunisia • One Note Samba • Satin Doll • Take the "A" Train • Yardbird Suite • and more.

00841438	Flute	$12.95
00841439	Clarinet	$12.95
00841440	Alto Sax	$12.95
00841441	Trumpet	$12.95
00841442	Tenor Sax	$12.95
00841443	Trombone	$12.95
00841444	Violin	$12.95

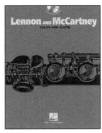

Lennon and McCartney Solos

11 favorites: All My Loving • Can't Buy Me Love • Eleanor Rigby • The Long and Winding Road • Ticket to Ride • Yesterday • and more.

00841542	Flute	$12.99
00841543	Clarinet	$12.99
00841544	Alto Sax	$12.99
00841545	Tenor Sax	$12.99
00841546	Trumpet	$12.99
00841547	Horn	$12.99
00841548	Trombone	$12.99
00841549	Violin	$12.99
00841625	Viola	$12.99
00841626	Cello	$12.99

Movie & TV Themes

12 favorite themes: A Whole New World • Where Everybody Knows Your Name • Moon River • Theme from Schindler's List • Theme from Star Trek® • You Must Love Me • and more.

00841452	Flute	$10.95
00841453	Clarinet	$10.95
00841454	Alto Sax	$10.95
00841455	Tenor Sax	$10.95
00841456	Trumpet	$10.95
00841458	Violin	$10.95

Sound of Music

9 songs: Climb Ev'ry Mountain • Do-Re-Mi • Edelweiss • The Lonely Goatherd • Maria • My Favorite Things • Sixteen Going on Seventeen • So Long, Farewell • The Sound of Music.

00841582	Flute	$11.95
00841583	Clarinet	$11.95
00841584	Alto Sax	$11.95
00841585	Tenor Sax	$11.95
00841586	Trumpet	$11.95
00841587	Horn	$11.95
00841588	Trombone	$11.95
00841589	Violin	$11.95
00841590	Viola	$11.95
00841591	Cello	$11.95

Worship Solos

11 top worship songs: Come, Now Is the Time to Worship • Draw Me Close • Firm Foundation • I Could Sing of Your Love Forever • Open the Eyes of My Heart • Shout to the North • and more.

00841836	Flute	$12.95
00841838	Clarinet	$12.95
00841839	Alto Sax	$12.95
00841840	Tenor Sax	$12.95
00841841	Trumpet	$12.95
00841843	Trombone	$12.95
00841844	Violin	$12.95
00841845	Viola	$12.95
00841846	Cello	$12.95